Oh, the doors you will open!

HARCOURT SCHOOL PUBLISHERS
STORYtown

Reach for the Stars

Senior Authors
Isabel L. Beck • Roger C. Farr • Dorothy S. Strickland

Authors
Alma Flor Ada • Roxanne F. Hudson • Margaret G. McKeown
Robin C. Scarcella • Julie A. Washington

Consultants
F. Isabel Campoy • Tyrone C. Howard • David A. Monti

Harcourt
SCHOOL PUBLISHERS

www.harcourtschool.com

ISBN 10 0-15-352168-6
ISBN 13 978-0-15-352168-3

3 4 5 6 7 8 9 10 751 16 15 14 13 12 11 10 09 08

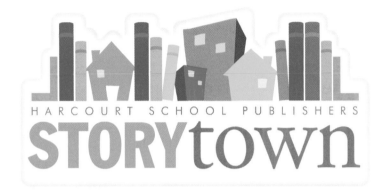

Reach for the Stars

Harcourt

SCHOOL PUBLISHERS

www.harcourtschool.com

Theme **4**
Wild and Wonderful

Contents

Paired Selections

Science

Science

4

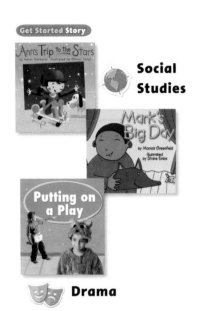

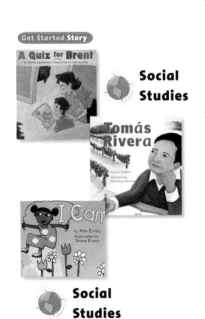

Lesson 18

Social Studies

Social Studies

Paired Selections

Theme Big Books

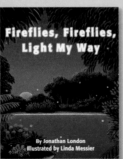

WE'RE GOING ON A LION HUNT — David Axtell

Fireflies, Fireflies, Light My Way — By Jonathan London, Illustrated by Linda Messier

READERS' THEATER — Practice Book

"Help Yourself"

Decodable Books 13–18

Comprehension Strategies

Before You Read

Look at the pictures. Think about what you already know.

Set a purpose.

I want to find out about frogs.

9

While You Read

Ask questions.

What do frogs eat?

Reread.

I'll read this page again.

Answer questions.

Oh! Some frogs eat bugs.

After You Read

Summarize.

First, tadpoles hatch from eggs. Then, they begin changing into frogs. Last, they are full-grown frogs.

Make connections.

This is like another book I read. I learned about how butterflies change.

Theme **4** Wild and Wonderful

Boy Playing with Toys, Steve Dininno

13

Contents

Lesson 13

1 Get Started Story

Rich Gets Big
by Sandra Widener • photographs by Steve Williams

2 Genre: Nonfiction

A Butterfly Grows
by Stephen Swinburne

Caterpillars
by Aileen Fisher
illustrated by Roberta Arenson

3 Genre: Poetry

Phonics
Words with <u>ch</u> and <u>tch</u>

Words to Know

Review

be

grow

was

Rich Gets Big

by Sandra Widener
photographs by Steve Williams

16

Rich has a wish to be big.

Rich stands to get a branch. He cannot get it.

"Grow just an inch more!" Mom calls.

Rich wants to pitch and catch. He cannot see the mitt on his shelf. Mom tells Rich, "You will not be small for long."

Rich sits on his porch
with his cat Patch. He
thinks he will not grow.

Mom brings Rich a chest with snapshots. Mom was small. Now she is big.

"I will grow!" thinks Rich.
Will Rich get that branch? Yes!
Will Rich get that mitt? Yes!

Focus Skill

 ## Sequence

Many stories and nonfiction selections tell about things in the order in which they happen—first, next, and last. This order is called the **sequence**.

Look at the pictures.

They show a sequence of first, next, and last.

Look at the pictures. Do the pictures show a sequence? What happens first, next, and last?

Try This!

Look at these pictures. Put the pictures in order. Tell what happens first, next, and last.

 www.harcourtschool.com/storytown

FCAT ✓ SS BENCHMARKS
LA.1.1.7.6 sequence events; LA.1.1.7.7 identify text structures

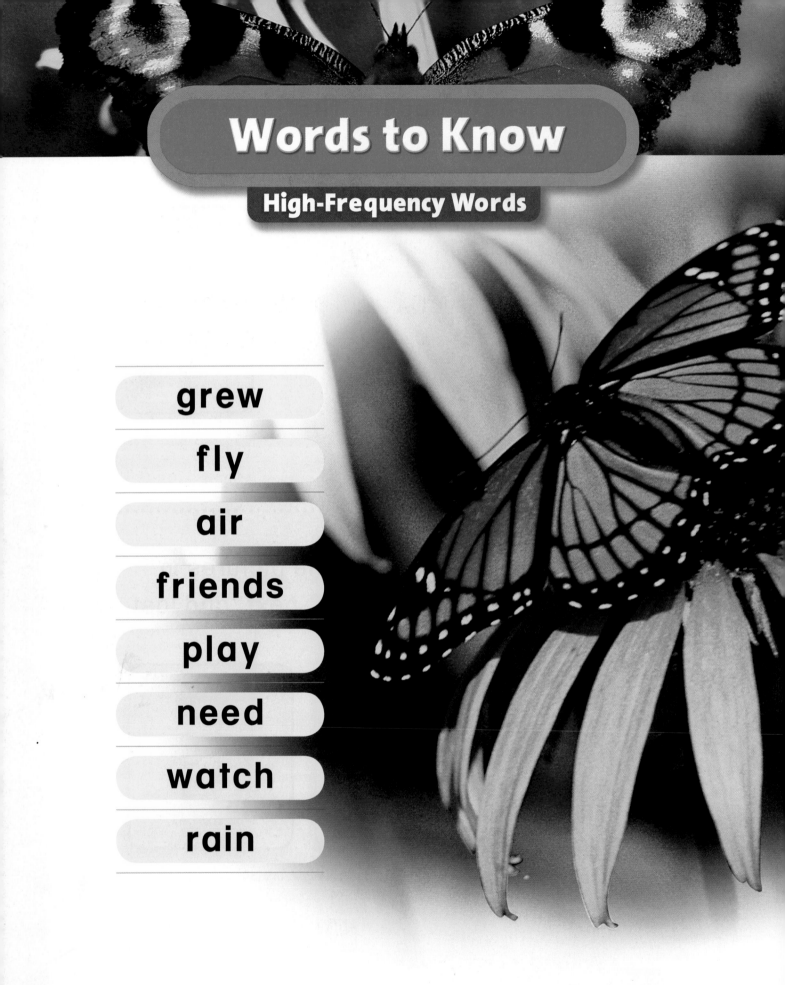

Words to Know

High-Frequency Words

grew

fly

air

friends

play

need

watch

rain

I **grew** from a small egg. Now I **fly** in the **air** with all my **friends**. Wings help us fly and **play**.

We **need** to drink water. We **watch** for **rain**. Then we sip drops on the plants.

 www.harcourtschool.com/storytown

A
Butterfly
Grows
by Stephen
Swinburne

Nonfiction

LA.1.1.7.6 **Genre Study**

Nonfiction selections tell about things that are true. They tell the order in which things happen.

```
┌─────────────────────────┐
│                         │
└─────────────────────────┘
            ↓
┌─────────────────────────┐
│                         │
└─────────────────────────┘
            ↓
┌─────────────────────────┐
│                         │
└─────────────────────────┘
            ↓
┌─────────────────────────┐
│                         │
└─────────────────────────┘
```

LA.1.2.2.3 **Comprehension Strategy**

 Use Graphic Organizers

As you read, use a graphic organizer like this to help you understand and remember information in the correct order.

FCAT ✓ SS BENCHMARKS
LA.1.1.7.6 sequence events; LA.1.2.2.3 organize information in non-fiction text

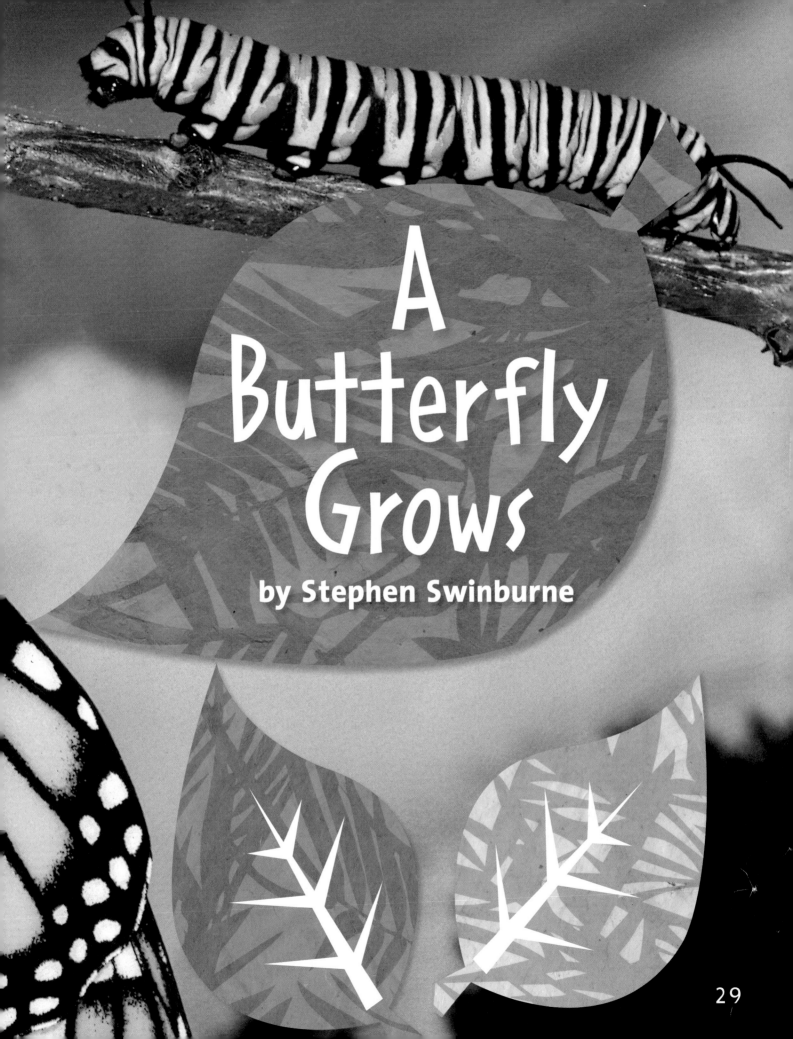

A Butterfly Grows

by Stephen Swinburne

Can you see me
on the plant?

I am a little caterpillar!
I grew in an egg.
Then I hatched!

Wind fills the air. I hang
onto a branch so I don't fall.

Rain falls. It plips and plops.
I need to drink water.
I drink the small drops.

This plant is my food. I need food so I can grow.

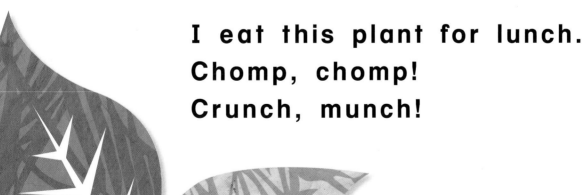

I eat this plant for lunch.
Chomp, chomp!
Crunch, munch!

I eat and grow,
eat and grow.
Now I am big!
My skin is snug.

I look for a spot to rest.
Soon I will shed my skin.

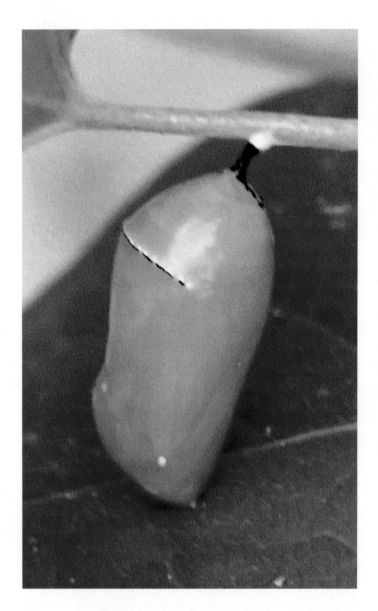

At last I am a chrysalis.
I'm an inch long.
Then in ten days, out I come!

Look at me now!
I am an insect.
I have six legs.

My wings help me fly.
Watch me fly!

I like to fly with all my friends.
Wings help us play.
Wings help us to go find plants for food.

Watch me eat now!
I sip and sip.

I am a butterfly!
I'm a beautiful butterfly!

43

Think Critically

1 How does the caterpillar change in this story? SEQUENCE

2 Why does the caterpillar eat so much? DETAILS

3 Why does the caterpillar come out of its chrysalis? DRAW CONCLUSIONS

4 Why do you think the author has the butterfly tell its own story?

AUTHOR'S PURPOSE

5 READ THINK EXPLAIN **WRITE** Imagine that you are a caterpillar or a butterfly for a day. Write about what you do.

WRITING RESPONSE

FCAT ✓ **SS BENCHMARKS**
LA.1.1.7.2 use background knowledge/supporting details;
LA.1.1.7.4 identify supporting details; LA.1.1.7.6 sequence events;
LA.1.1.7.8 identify author's purpose; LA.1.2.1.5 respond to texts;
LA.1.4.2.1 write informational/expository forms

Meet the Author/Photographer
Stephen Swinburne

Stephen Swinburne loves nature—especially butterflies! He planted a garden at his house filled with flowers that butterflies like. He took many of the pictures for "A Butterfly Grows" in his garden. He hopes you enjoy learning about butterflies!

GO online www.harcourtschool.com/storytown

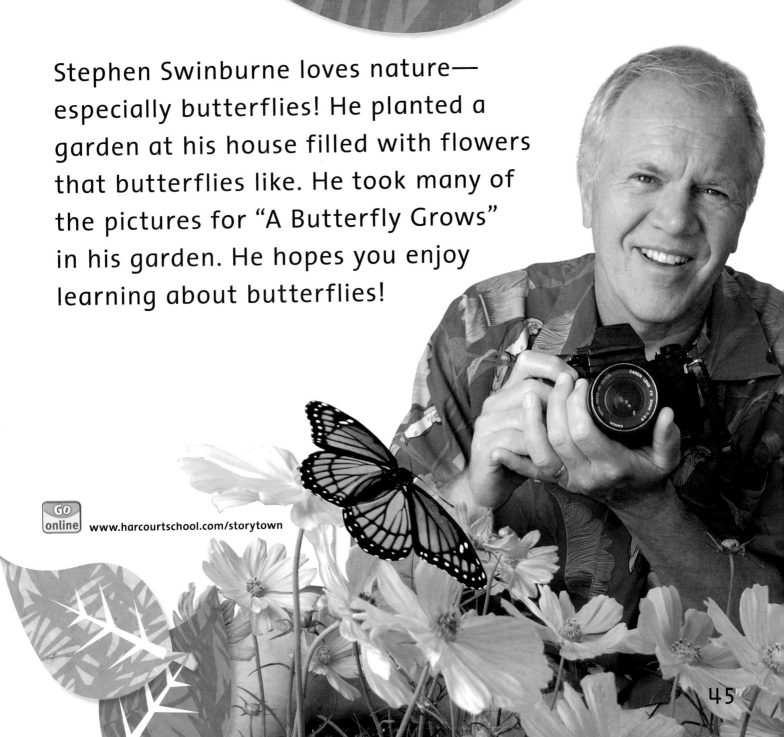

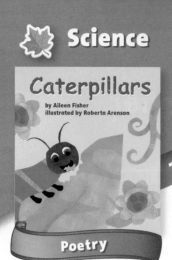

Caterpillars

by Aileen Fisher

illustrated by Roberta Arenson

What do caterpillars do?
Nothing much but chew and chew.

What do caterpillars know?
Nothing much but how to grow.

They just eat what by and by
will make them be a butterfly,

But that is more than I can do
however much I chew and chew.

Connections

Comparing Texts LA.1.1.7.2 LA.1.1.7.4 LA.1.2.1.5

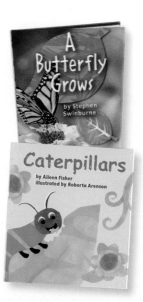

1 What do the story and the poem say a caterpillar must do to grow?

2 Tell about a butterfly or another bug you have seen. What did it do?

3 How have you changed as you have grown?

Writing LA.1.1.7.6 LA.1.2.2.3 LA.1.4.2.1

Think about the story. Write three sentences to tell how a butterfly grows.

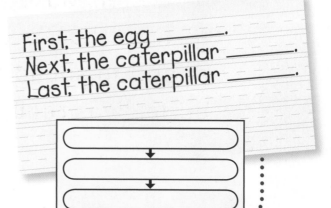

First, the egg _____.
Next, the caterpillar _____.
Last, the caterpillar _____.

Phonics LA.1.1.4.1

Make and read new words.

Start with **<u>chin</u>**.

Switch **c** **h** and **i** **n** .

Add **p** in front of **i** .

Change **n** to **t** .

Change **i** to **a** .

Fluency Practice LA.1.1.5.1 LA.1.1.5.2

Read the story aloud with a partner. Make your voice go up or down. Make it loud or soft to sound as if the butterfly is really talking.

I am a butterfly!

I'm a beautiful butterfly!

FCAT ✓ SS BENCHMARKS
LA.1.1.4.1 generate/blend sounds into words; LA.1.1.5.1 apply letter-sound knowledge to decode quickly and accurately;
LA.1.1.5.2 recognize high-frequency/familiar words; LA.1.1.7.2 use background knowledge/supporting details; LA.1.1.7.4 identify
supporting details; LA.1.1.7.6 sequence events; LA.1.2.1.5 respond to texts; LA.1.2.2.3 organize information in non-fiction text;
LA.1.4.2.1 write informational/expository forms

Reading-Writing Connection

Responding to a Selection

"A Butterfly Grows" is a nonfiction selection about how butterflies grow and change. We read the selection. Then we wrote about what we knew and what we learned.

▶ **First, we talked about the selection.**

▶ **Next, we named things we already knew and things we learned.**

▶ **Last, we read our sentences.**

What We Knew
Caterpillars change into butterflies.

Butterflies have six legs.

What We Learned
Caterpillars eat leaves and drink drops of water.

A butterfly is in a chrysalis for ten days.

Contents

Lesson 14

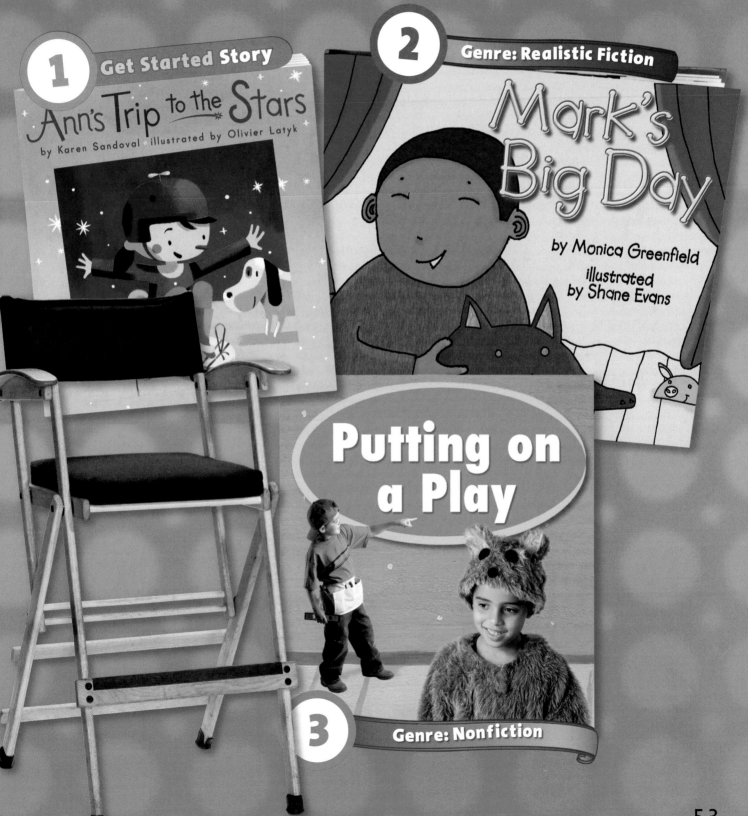

1 Get Started Story

Ann's Trip to the Stars
by Karen Sandoval illustrated by Olivier Latyk

2 Genre: Realistic Fiction

Mark's Big Day
by Monica Greenfield
illustrated by Shane Evans

Putting on a Play

3 Genre: Nonfiction

Phonics

Words with <u>ar</u>

Words to Know

Review

play

says

her

cold

Ann's Trip
to the Stars

by Karen Sandoval

illustrated by Olivier Latyk

54

"Dad, will you help with my play?" asks Ann.

"Yes!" says Dad.

55

Dad hangs cloth in the hall.

"I am off to the stars!" grins Ann.
"My ship will go far in a flash."

56

Ann starts her long trip.
"The sun is big and hot," says Ann.
"Mars is red. It can get cold."

"My ship will not start," says Ann.

Bark! Bark!

"Carl has a kit to fix it!"

60

Dad claps. Mom claps. Ben stands
and claps, and Carl barks.
"Thanks!" says Ann with a big grin.

Phonics Skill

Words with **ar**

The letters **ar** can stand for the sound at the beginning of the words **art** and **arm**.

art   arm

The letters **ar** can stand for the same sound in the middle of **yarn** and at the end of **star**.

yarn   star

Look at each picture. Read the words.
Tell which word names the picture.

card

cart

cord

scar

sort

scarf

GO online   www.harcourtschool.com/storytown

Try This!

Read the story.

We went to a farm in the car. It was very far. We saw animals at the barn. We went on a cart. At night, we saw some stars.

feel

put

house

Mrs.

say

loud

again

know

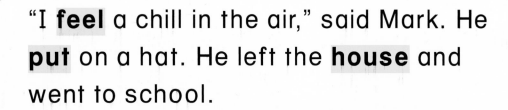

"I **feel** a chill in the air," said Mark. He **put** on a hat. He left the **house** and went to school.

At school, **Mrs.** Parks said, "**Say** your part, Mark. Be **loud**." Mark said his part.

"Now say it **again**. I **know** you can do a good job!" she said.

GO online www.harcourtschool.com/storytown

Mark's Big Day
by Monica Greenfield
illustrated by Shane Evans

Realistic Fiction

LA.1.2.1.1
LA.1.2.1.2
LA.1.2.1.3

Genre Study

Realistic fiction stories are made-up, but have characters like people we know.

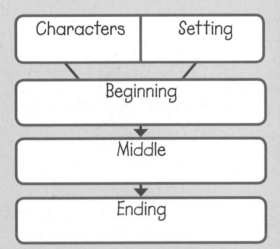

Characters	Setting

Beginning

Middle

Ending

Comprehension

LA.1.1.7.3

Strategy

Summarize As you read, stop every few pages and think about the important things that have happened so far.

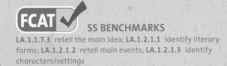

FCAT ✓ **SS BENCHMARKS**

LA.1.1.7.3 retell the main idea; LA.1.2.1.1 identify literary forms; LA.1.2.1.2 retell main events; LA.1.2.1.3 identify characters/settings

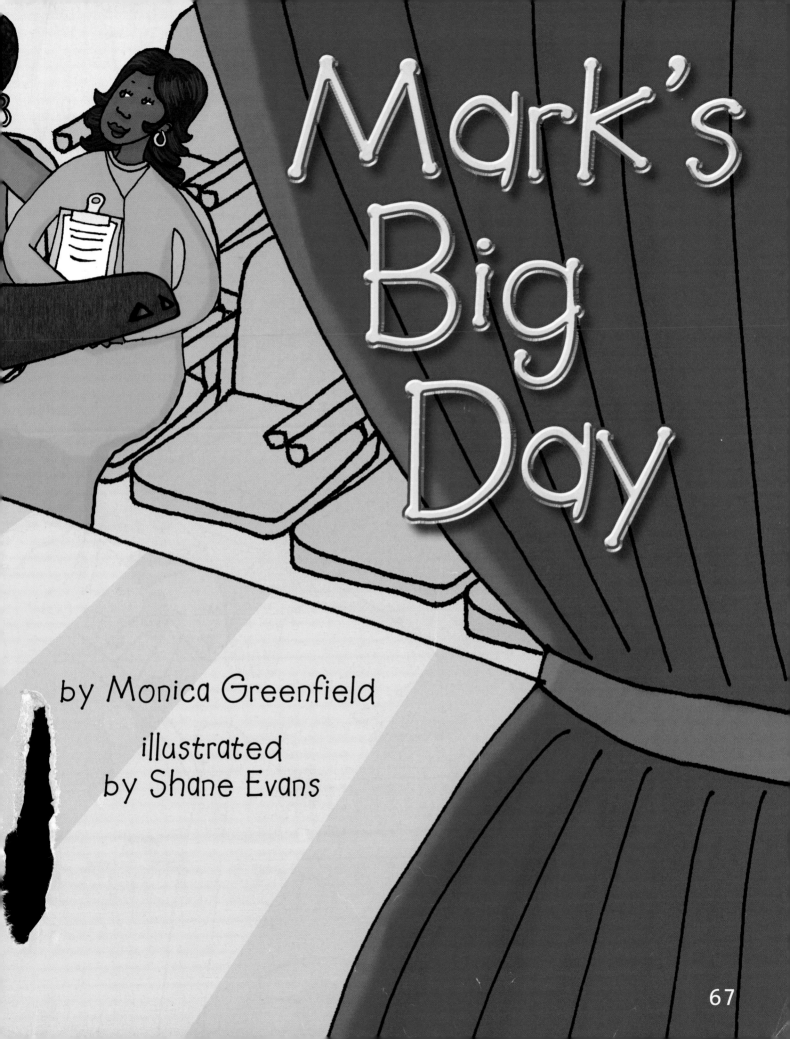

Mark's
Big
Day

by Monica Greenfield

illustrated
by Shane Evans

Mark's clock went <u>bing</u>, <u>bing</u>, <u>bing</u>.
He did not want to get up.

Bing! Bing! Bing!

68

Mom called, "Mark, get up and get dressed. It's your big day!"

Mark was thinking of the school play.
His part was hard for him. He felt shy.
Mark put on his jacket, hat, and scarf.

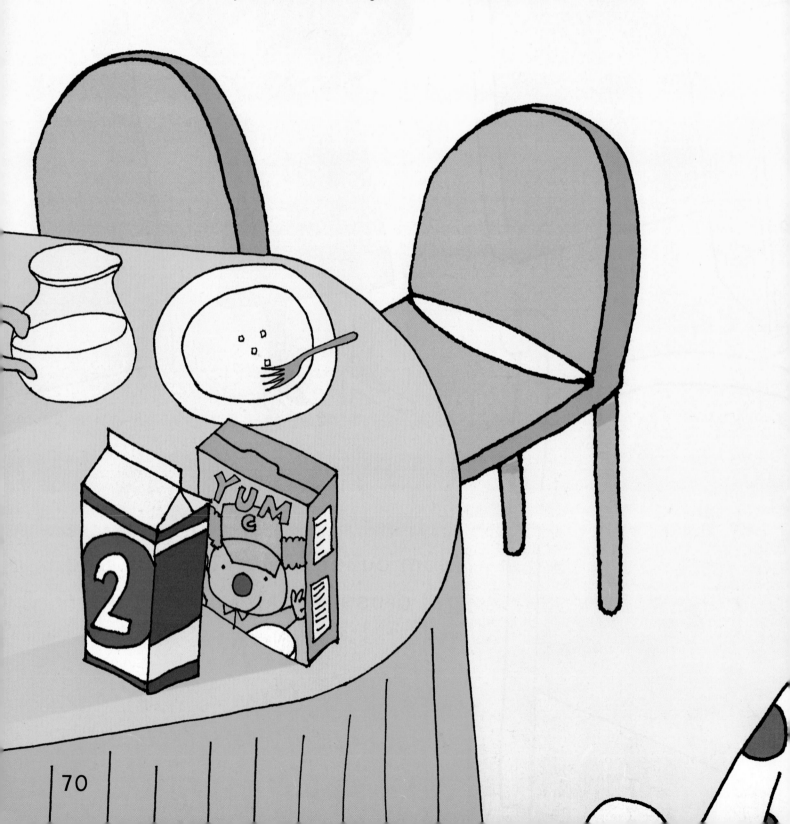

"Wish me luck," Mark said. He got a big hug from Mom. His dog barked.
"Thanks, Mom. Thanks, Champ," Mark said with a grin.

At school, Mrs. Parks asked
the children to say their parts.

73

"I'll huff and I'll puff and I'll blow your house in," Mark said. It was too soft.

"Say it again, Mark," Mrs. Parks called.
"I'll blow your house in," Mark said.
It was soft again.

"You are the wolf. This wolf is not shy," said Mrs. Parks.

"This is hard, but I know you can do it, Mark. Just act like a big wolf."

The play started. Soon it was time for Mark to say his part.

"I'll huff and I'll puff and I'll blow
your house OUT!" he called.

The children looked at Mark.
He had made a mistake.

Three Pigs' House

"Oh! I'll huff and I'll puff and I'll blow your house IN!" Mark said with a big wolf snarl.

"Don't feel bad, Mark,"
Mrs. Parks said.

"I don't," Mark said. "I feel good."
"You do?" asked Mrs. Parks.

"Yes! I wasn't shy. I was LOUD!"
Mark said with a big grin.

84

Think Critically

1 What do you think the author wanted you to learn from the story?

AUTHOR'S PURPOSE/POINT OF VIEW

2 Who helps Mark at home? Who helps Mark at school? DETAILS

3 Why do you think Mark says his part softly at first? MAKE INFERENCES

4 Why is Mark able to say his part loudly during the play? DRAW CONCLUSIONS

5 READ THINK EXPLAIN **WRITE** Write about how you would act as the wolf in a play. What kind of costume would you wear? WRITING RESPONSE

FCAT ✓ **SS BENCHMARKS**
LA.1.1.7.2 use background knowledge/supporting details; LA.1.1.7.4 identify supporting details; LA.1.1.7.8 identify author's purpose; LA.1.2.1.5 respond to texts; LA.1.4.2.1 write informational/expository forms

85

Meet the Author
Monica Greenfield

Monica Greenfield comes from a family of writers. Her mother writes stories and poems, and so did her grandmother. Her daughter loves to write, also.

"Words can be very powerful. I can use words to make children laugh, give them something to think about, or let them know how strong they are."

Meet the Illustrator

Shane Evans

Shane Evans has illustrated many children's books. He has created art for people all over the world. His art has been shown in Africa, Paris, New York, and Chicago. Mr. Evans also likes to speak at schools. He encourages children to use their own special talents.

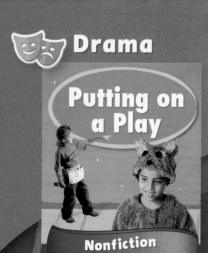

Putting on
a Play

Nonfiction

Putting on a Play

Many people work together to put on a play.

The **Director** is in charge. He or she tells everyone what to do.

The Three Bears
Putting on a Play

The **Set Designer** is in charge of how the stage will look for the play.

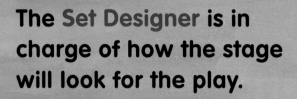

Actors and Actresses need to know how to pretend. They use words and actions to tell a story.

The **Costume Designer** makes the clothes that the actors and actresses wear.

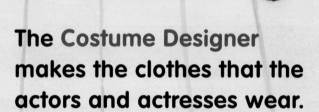

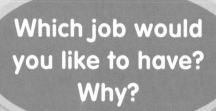

Which job would you like to have? Why?

89

Connections

Comparing Texts LA.1.2.1.5

1 What job from "Putting on a Play" do you think Mark would like? Why?

2 Tell what you liked about Mark's play or about a play you have seen.

3 What would you tell a friend who felt shy or afraid?

Writing LA.1.4.2.1

Mark felt proud of himself. Write about something you have done that you are proud of.

I am proud of how I take care of my baby brother.

Make and read new words.

Start with **far**.

Add **m** to the end.

Take away the **f**.

Change **m** to **t**.

Add **p** to the beginning.

Read the story aloud with a partner. Read softly where Mark speaks softly. Read like the Big Bad Wolf where Mark does!

I'll huff and I'll puff . . .

SS BENCHMARKS

LA.1.1.4.1 generate/blend sounds into words; **LA.1.1.5.1** apply letter-sound knowledge to decode quickly and accurately; **LA.1.1.5.2** recognize high-frequency/familiar words; **LA.1.2.1.5** respond to texts; **LA.1.4.2.1** write informational/expository forms

Contents

Lesson 15

1 Get Started Story

A Quiz for Brent

by Karen Sandoval • illustrated by Joe Cepeda

2 Genre: Biography

Tomás Rivera

by Jane Medina

illustrated by
René King Moreno

3 I Can

by Mari Evans
illustrated by
Shane Evans

Genre: Poetry

Phonics
Words with <u>qu</u>

Words to Know

Review

happy

too

find

house

A Quiz for Brent

by Karen Sandoval

illustrated by

Joe Cepeda

Mom has a quiz for Brent.
Brent gets a hint. "Check the
bed, Brent," Mom tells him.

Think, Brent, think!
A small, red bucket is
on the soft quilt. Brent
is glad he got that hint.

96

Dad has a quiz for Brent.
Brent gets a hint.

"Check the desk, Brent,"
Dad tells him.

Think, Brent, think!
A big, tan cloth is on the
desk. Brent is happy he got
that hint, too.

What will Brent find? Is it Mom?
Is it Dad? Brent will finish his
quiz out of the house.

Brent will not quit.
He runs to the yard!
Quick, Brent, quick!

100

It's Granddad! Brent is glad he did not quit!

Focus Skill

Sequence

Authors tell about things in the order in which they happen. The order makes sense. This order is called the **sequence**.

Look at the pictures.

They show a sequence of first, next, and last.

Look at the pictures. Do they show a sequence? What happens first, next, and last?

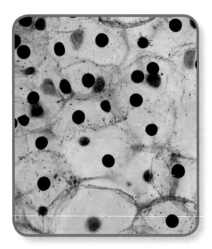  

Try This!

Look at these pictures. Put them in order. Tell what happens first, next, and last.

 www.harcourtschool.com/storytown

FCAT ✓ SS BENCHMARKS
LA.1.1.7.6 sequence events; LA.1.1.7.7 identify text structures

103

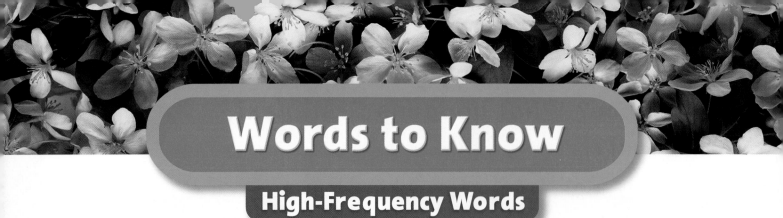

Words to Know

High-Frequency Words

books

about

read

work

writing

people

family

name

I have **books about** cars and trucks. It is fun to **read** lots of books.

I like to **work** on stories, too. I am **writing** one to tell **people** about my **family**. It is hard work, but I like it! I will put my **name** on it.

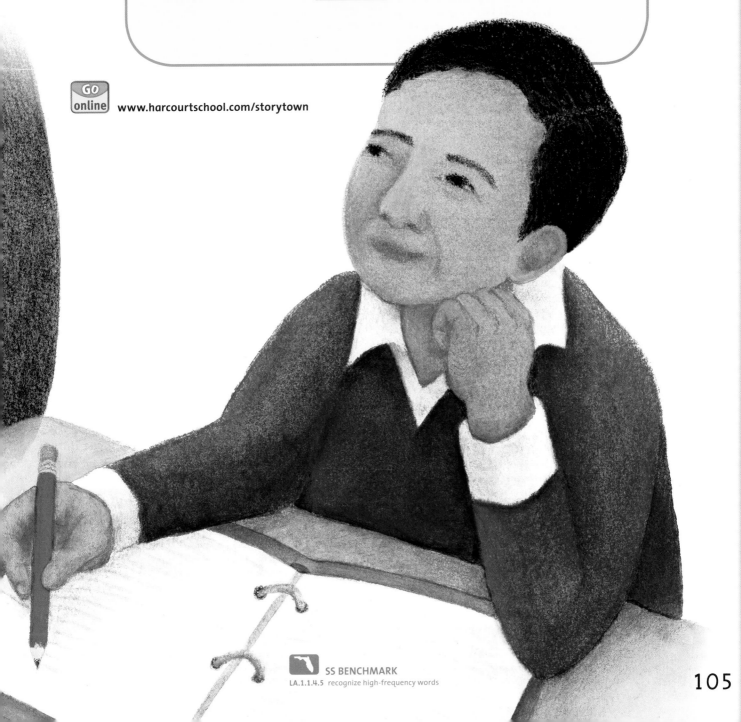

GO online www.harcourtschool.com/storytown

Tomás Rivera

by Jane Medina
illustrated by
René King Moreno

Biography

Award Winner

LA.1.2.2.3 **Genre Study**
A **biography** is a story about the events in the life of a real person.

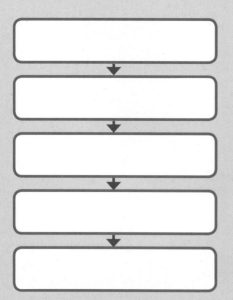

LA.1.1.7.8 **Comprehension Strategy**

Ask Questions As you read, ask yourself questions and look for the answers.

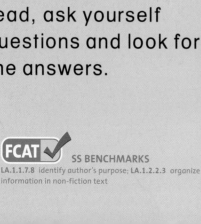

FCAT ✓ SS BENCHMARKS
LA.1.1.7.8 identify author's purpose; LA.1.2.2.3 organize information in non-fiction text

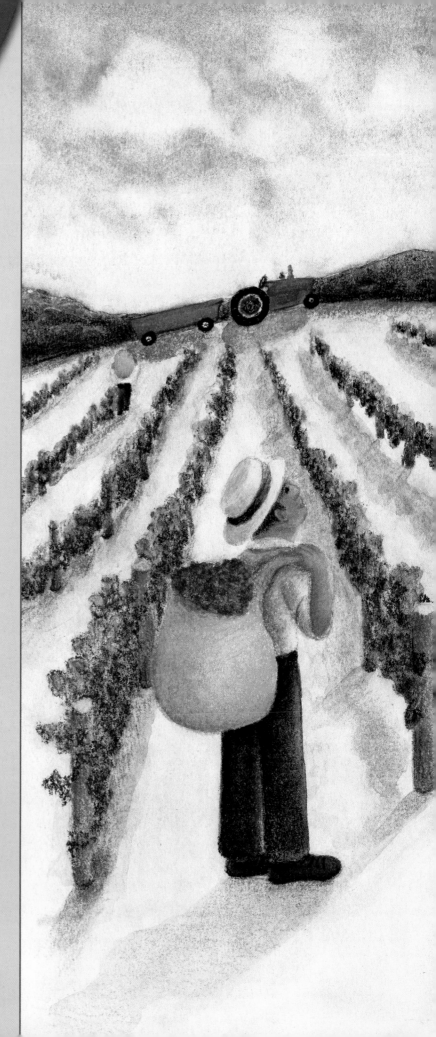

Tomás Rivera

by Jane Medina

illustrated by
René King Moreno

Tomás Rivera was born in Texas.
Tomás and his family went from
farm to farm picking crops.

Tomás helped pick crops all day.
It was hard work. At night he had
fun with his Grandpa.

"Come quick, children!" Grandpa called.
"It's time for stories!"

"You tell the best stories!"
Tomás said. "I want to tell
good stories, too."

"We can get lots of stories
for you, Tomás," said Grandpa.
"When?" asked Tomás.

"Let's go now!" Grandpa said with a wink. "Quick, hop in!"

"This is a library," said Grandpa.
"Look at all the books!" gasped
Tomás as he clapped his hands.

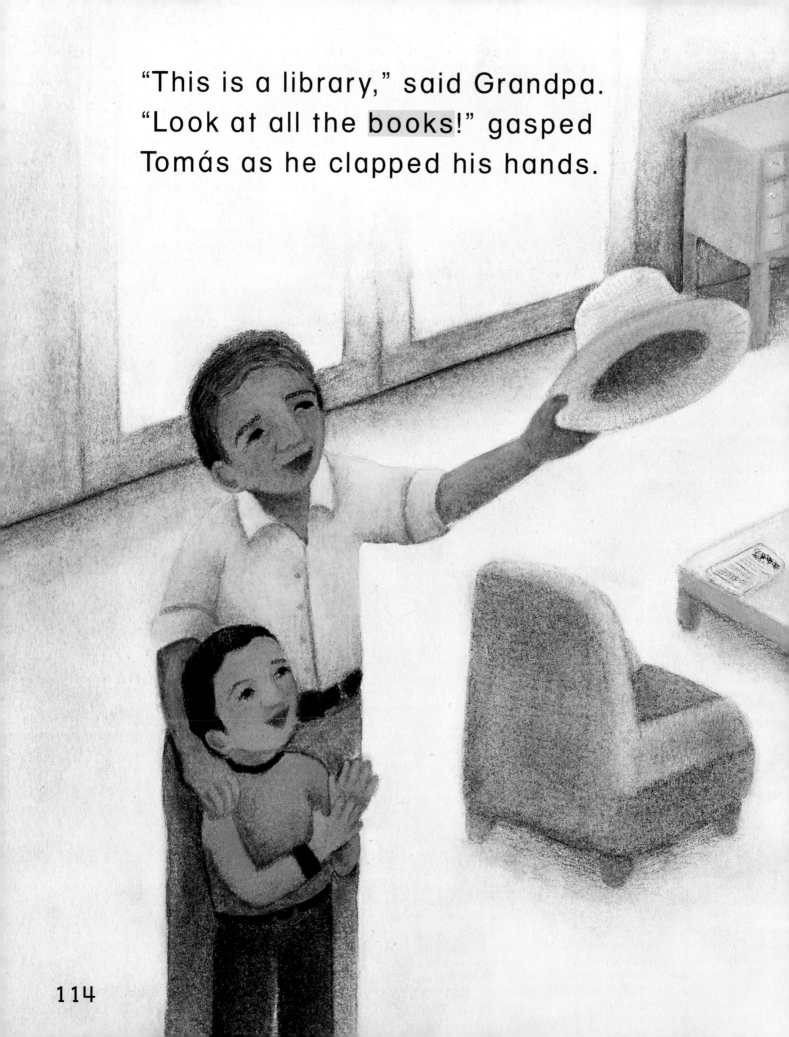

"Read all you can, Tomás. It will
help you think of lots of stories,"
said Grandpa.

Tomás read lots and lots of books.
He read about bugs, stars, and cars.
Tomás started thinking of stories.

Tomás started telling his stories.
Then he started writing them.

When he grew up, Tomás got
a job as a teacher. He still
kept writing stories.

Tomás Rivera's stories tell about people picking crops, just as his family did. Lots of people read his books.

Now his name is on a big library.
Many people visit the library.
They get books, just as Tomás did.

Think Critically

1 How does Tomás feel about books after he goes to the library with Grandpa?  SEQUENCE

2 Why does Grandpa want Tomás to read lots of books? MAKE INFERENCES

3 How does Tomás learn to tell stories? PLOT

4 Why do you think Tomás Rivera wrote stories about people picking crops? DRAW CONCLUSIONS

5  **WRITE** Write about a job you would like to have someday.

✐ WRITING RESPONSE

FCAT ✓ SS BENCHMARKS
LA.1.1.7.2 use background knowledge/supporting details; **LA.1.1.7.4** identify supporting details; **LA.1.1.7.7** identify text structures; **LA.1.2.1.2** retell main events; **LA.1.2.1.5** respond to texts; **LA.1.4.2.1** write informational/expository forms

Meet the Author
Jane Medina

Jane Medina read a lot about Tomás Rivera so that she could tell this story about his life. She hopes the story will help children think as Tomás Rivera did.

❝If you work hard and do well in school, you can do anything you want to do!❞

Meet the Illustrator
René King Moreno

When René King Moreno was young, she loved to spend her spare time drawing and painting. She studied art in school, and now she illustrates children's books.

GO online www.harcourtschool.com/storytown

123

I Can
by Mari Evans
illustrated by
Shane Evans

Poetry

by Mari Evans
illustrated by
Shane Evans

I Can

I can
be anything
I can
do anything
I can
think
anything
big
or tall
OR
high or low
W I D E
or narrow
fast or slow
because I
CAN
and
I
WANT
TO!

Connections

Comparing Texts LA.1.2.1.3 LA.1.2.1.5

1 How is Tomás like the girl in the poem "I Can"?

2 Why is it important to believe you can do the things you want to do?

3 What things did Tomás do that you also like to do?

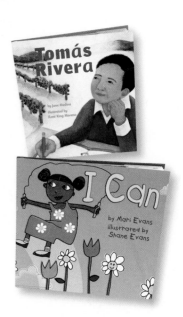

Writing LA.1.4.1.1

Write about something special you did with a family member or friend. Tell what happened first, next, and last.

> One day, my dad and I went to the park. We played basketball together. I won! Then we ate ice cream cones. It was fun!

Make and read new words.

Start with **quick**.

Change **i** to **a**.

Change **q** **u** to **w** **h**.

Change **c** **k** to **t**.

Change **a** **t** to **e** **n**.

Fluency Practice LA.1.1.5.1 LA.1.1.5.2 LA.1.1.5.3

Read "Tomás Rivera" with a classmate. Take turns reading the pages. Read the easy parts quickly. Read the harder parts more slowly.

FCAT ✓ SS BENCHMARKS

LA.1.1.4.1 generate/blend sounds into words; **LA.1.1.5.1** apply letter-sound knowledge to decode quickly and accurately;
LA.1.1.5.2 recognize high-frequency/familiar words; **LA.1.1.5.3** adjust reading rate; **LA.1.2.1.3** identify characters/settings;
LA.1.2.1.5 respond to texts; **LA.1.4.1.1** write narratives

Contents

Lesson 16

1 Get Started Story

A Perfect Lunch

by Karen Sandoval   illustrated by Victoria Raymond

2 Genre: Fantasy

One More Friend

retold by Alma Flor Ada
illustrated by Sophie Fatus

Good Friends

3 Genre: Nonfiction

A Perfect Lunch

by Karen Sandoval
illustrated by
Victoria Raymond

"Come for lunch," says Meg.
She is serving corn muffins.
Meg sets out her best dishes.
"How charming!" she grins.

Ben comes first. He sits
with Meg. Ben fills his glass.
Squirt! He squirts Meg.
"Oh, no!" yells Ben.

Liz is next. She sits with Ben.
Liz picks up her muffin, and her
skirt bumps Ben.

Kit is third. She sits with Liz. Kit sips
her drink and drops her muffin in the
dirt. Meg's big hat brim hits Ben.

Here is Jen. Where can this bird sit? Perhaps this twig will do the trick. Liz looks up and bumps Meg's hat.

Tap, tap, tap! It's Bert!

"Oh, no! Where will Bert sit?"
they all ask.

"Let's have a picnic!" says Bert.

"It's a perfect day now with all my friends," Meg says. Meg and all her friends have a perfect lunch!

Focus Skill

 Main Idea

What a story is mostly about is the **main idea**.

Look at the picture.

The main idea is that a family is having dinner.

Look at the picture. What is the main idea? How do you know?

Try This!

Look at this picture. Tell what you think the main idea is.

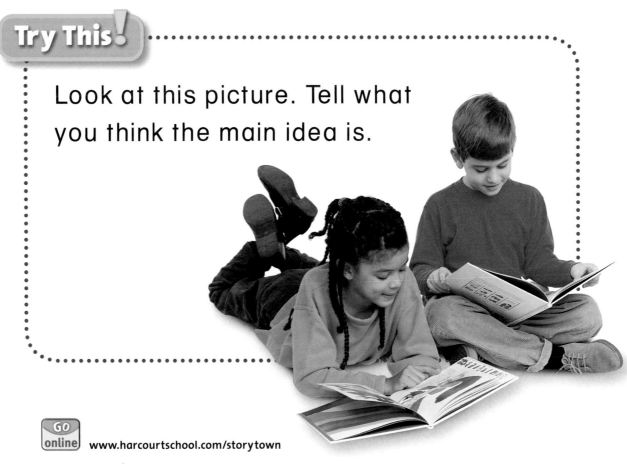

GO online www.harcourtschool.com/storytown

FCAT ✓ SS BENCHMARKS
LA.1.1.7.3 retell the main idea; LA.1.2.1.2 retell main events

Words to Know

Cow's

nice

by

please

join

always

room

Ant, Frog, and Chick like to be in **Cow's** yard. They think it's **nice** to sit **by** their friends. Here comes Hen.

"**Please** come and **join** us!" the animals say. They **always** make **room** for one more friend.

www.harcourtschool.com/storytown

Award-Winning Author and Illustrator

One More Friend

retold by Alma Flor Ada
illustrated by Sophie Fatus

Fantasy

LA.1.2.1.1 Genre Study

A **fantasy** is a story that has make-believe characters and events.

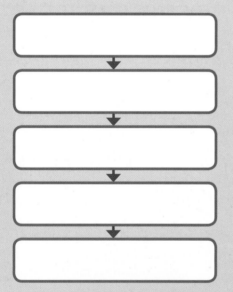

Comprehension
LA.1.1.7.3 Strategy

Summarize As you read, stop every few pages and think about the important things that have happened so far.

One More Friend

retold by Alma Flor Ada

illustrated by Sophie Fatus

"My, it's nice to rest in the shade!"
Ant is happy in the hammock in Cow's
backyard.

144

Frog hops up. "Ribbit ribbit!"
"Jump up, Frog! Be the first!" calls Ant.
"There's always room for one more.
Please don't say you can't!"

Chick skips by. "Chirp chirp!"
"Come join us, little bird!" calls Ant.
"There's always room for one more.
Please don't say you can't!"

Hen steps up. "Cluck cluck!"
"Come join us! Be the third!" calls Ant.
"There's always room for one more.
Please don't say you can't!"

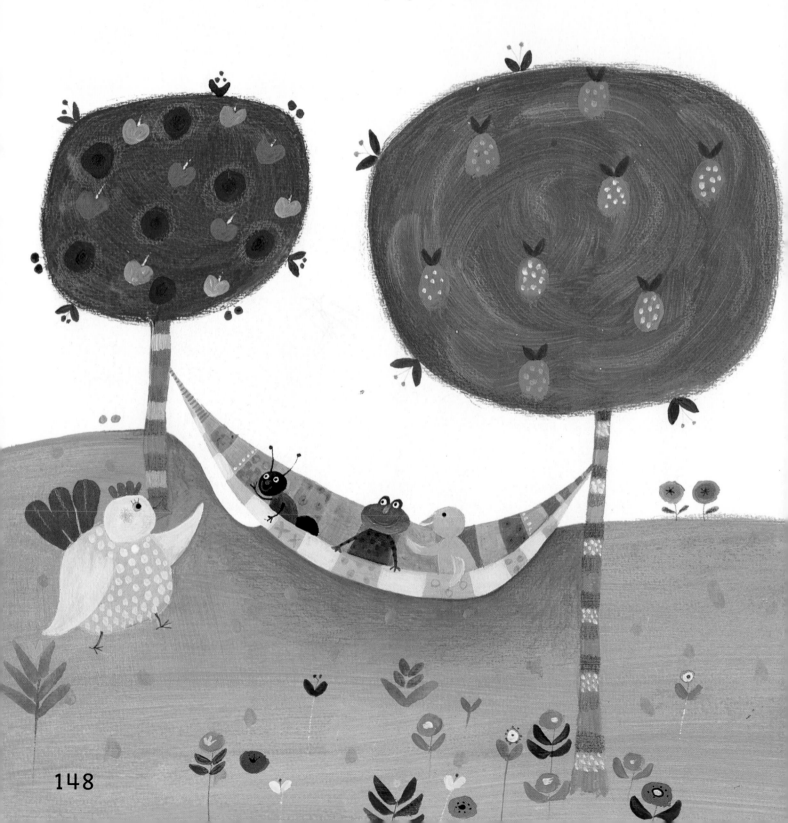

Duck flaps his wings. "Quack quack!"
"Come join us, good sir!" calls Ant.
"There's always room for one more.
Please don't say you can't!"

"My, it's nice to rest in the shade!"
Ant, Frog, Chick, Hen, and Duck are
all happy in the hammock in Cow's
backyard.

Cat slinks by in the grass. "Purr purr!"
"Come join us and curl up!" calls Ant.
"There's always room for one more.
Please don't say you can't!"

Dog and Lamb run up. "Bark bark! Baaa baaa!"
"Come join us! It's your turn!" calls Ant.
"There's always room for one more.
Please don't say you can't!"

"My, it's nice to rest in the shade!"
Ant, Frog, Chick, Hen, Duck, Cat, Dog,
and Lamb are all happy in the hammock
in Cow's backyard.

Then up jumps Cow.
Who is this now?
It's a big elephant!
What will Ant say?
Oh, no! She can't. . .

154

But Ant calls out,
"Come join us!"

When there is kindness,
there's always a way
for one more friend
to join in and play!

Think Critically

1. How does Ant show kindness?

   MAIN IDEA

2. What other animal in the story is kind? Why do you think so? DRAW CONCLUSIONS

3. Who does Ant invite into the hammock? DETAILS

4. What are the animals worried about when the elephant comes by? MAKE INFERENCES

5. READ THINK EXPLAIN **WRITE** Write about one way you can be kind to others. WRITING RESPONSE

FCAT ✓ **SS BENCHMARKS**
LA.1.1.7.2 use background knowledge/supporting details; **LA.1.1.7.3** retell the main idea; **LA.1.1.7.4** identify supporting details; **LA.1.2.1.5** respond to texts; **LA.1.4.2.1** write informational/expository forms

Meet the Author
Alma Flor Ada

The ideas for "One More Friend" come from Alma Flor Ada's childhood. She loved hammocks as a child in Cuba, and slept on them many times. Also, at her house they were always making room at the table for a relative or visitor. Her cousin would often say, "There's always room for one more!"

Meet the Illustrator
Sophie Fatus

Sophie Fatus is an artist who grew up in France and now lives in Italy. She loves animals and enjoys painting them very much, like the ones in this story. She hopes that her artwork will help children remember to like each other and be kind to one another.

GO online www.harcourtschool.com/storytown

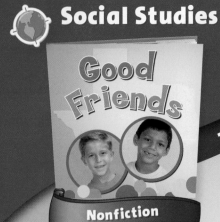

Good Friends

Luis lives in Dallas, Texas. Andy lives in Stonewall.

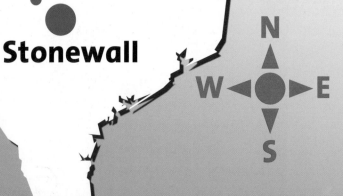

Dallas

Stonewall

N
W E
S

They are good friends even though they live far apart.

Luis likes living in Dallas because it has tall buildings and busy streets.

Andy likes living around the farms and wide open spaces in Stonewall.

Best of all, Luis and Andy like spending time together.

Connections

Comparing Texts LA.1.2.1.5

1 Did you like "One More Friend" or "Good Friends" better? Why?

2 Think of a person you know who is like Ant. How is this person like Ant?

3 How would you be kind to someone?

Writing LA.1.1.7.3 LA.1.1.7.4 LA.1.4.2.4

Write a note to invite a friend to your house. List the things you plan to do when he or she visits.

Main Idea
things to do for fun with my friend

Details

ride bikes

eat a snack

play with my dog

Phonics LA.1.1.4.1

Make and read new words.

Start with the word **sir**.

Change **s** to **b**. Add **d** to the end.

Change **b** to **t** **h**.

Take off **t**. Change **i** to **e**.

Change **e** to **u** and **d** to **t**.

Fluency Practice LA.1.1.5.1 LA.1.1.5.2 LA.1.1.5.3

Read "One More Friend" with a classmate. Read each sentence together. Read at a steady pace. Try to keep the rhythm of the words.

There's always room for one more.

Please don't say you can't!

FCAT ✓ SS BENCHMARKS

LA.1.1.4.1 generate/blend sounds into words; **LA.1.1.5.1** apply letter-sound knowledge to decode quickly and accurately; **LA.1.1.5.2** recognize high-frequency/familiar words; **LA.1.1.5.3** adjust reading rate; **LA.1.1.7.3** retell the main idea; **LA.1.1.7.4** identify supporting details; **LA.1.2.1.5** respond to texts; **LA.1.4.2.4** write basic communications (friendly letters, thank-you notes)

Contents

Lesson 17

1 Get Started **Story**

Jungle Fun

by Nancy Furstinger
illustrated by Michelle Angers

2 Genre: Nonfiction

Can Elephants Paint?

by Katya Arnold

3 An Elephant's Three T's

Genre: Nonfiction Article

Phonics

Words with le

Words to Know

Review

soon

animals

make

family

join

Jungle Fun

by Nancy Furstinger

illustrated by
Michelle Angers

A contest will start soon. The contest is in the jungle. The animals will do fun tricks. Who will win?

Big cats run and jump and tumble.
Little cats giggle and chuckle.

Big red foxes juggle balls and pins.
Little red foxes cannot catch the
balls and pins.

Big birds ring bells that jingle jangle. Little birds chirp and make bubbles.

An elephant family will join in the fun. They have purple hats that glitter and sparkle.

Big elephants stomp and kick.
Little elephants wiggle and turn
and spin.

Big animals and little animals all have fun! Who can do the best tricks?

You pick!

173

Focus Skill

 Main Idea

The **main idea** of a story is the most important idea.

Look at the picture.

The main idea is that a boy is learning to tie his shoes.

Look at the picture. What is the main idea? How do you know?

Try This!

Look at the picture. Choose the words that name the main idea.

- working on a farm
- working at school
- working at home

Go online www.harcourtschool.com/storytown

SS BENCHMARKS
LA.1.1.7.3 retell the main idea; LA.1.2.1.2 retell main events

Words to Know

High-Frequency Words

would

carry

other

money

buy

paint

paper

176

The elephants on a farm had jobs. They **would carry** trees with their trunks.

An artist met an elephant named Lucky. The artist liked Lucky and the **other** elephants on the farm.

The artist used **money** to **buy** things for the elephants. Now they have **paint**, brushes, and **paper**.

 www.harcourtschool.com/storytown

SS BENCHMARK
LA.1.1.4.5 recognize high-frequency words

Can Elephants Paint?
by Katya Arnold

Nonfiction

LA.1.1.7.3
LA.1.2.2.3 **Genre Study**

A **nonfiction** selection gives true information about a main idea. It often has photographs.

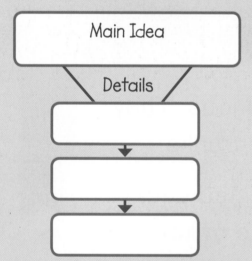

Main Idea

Details

Comprehension

LA.1.1.7.9 **Strategy**

Monitor Comprehension: Reread If you read a part that you don't understand, go back and read it again.

 SS BENCHMARKS
LA.1.1.7.3 retell the main idea; LA.1.1.7.9 self monitor; reread;
LA.1.2.2.3 organize information in non-fiction text

178

Can Elephants Paint?

a true story by Katya Arnold

Lucky lived on a farm.
She was big and strong.

All the elephants on that farm had jobs. They worked in the jungle.

Ning worked with Lucky. Ning cut trees. Then Lucky would carry them off with her trunk.

Ning and Lucky worked hard to get money.

On days off, they would swim.

One day, all the big trees were cut. There were no more jobs. "What will we do?" asked Ning.

An artist had a good idea.
"I think I can help them," she
said. The artist went to the farm.

"I use my hands when I paint. Elephants can use their trunks," said the artist. She dipped a brush in purple.

Lucky grabbed the handle
with her trunk.
"Good!" said the artist. "Let's
paint, Lucky!"

Lucky made a little spot.
The artist started to giggle.
"Not on your head, darling!
Watch me."

The artist dragged the brush on the
paper. Then she handed it back to
Lucky. Lucky blinked.
"You can do it!" said the artist.

Lucky made a little purple
dot in the middle.
"You are an artist, Lucky!"

Then the artist held Lucky's trunk.
She helped Lucky paint lines, wiggles,
splashes, and little dots.

Other elephants came by.
The artist handed them all
brushes.

"How can this help us get
money?" Ning was thinking.

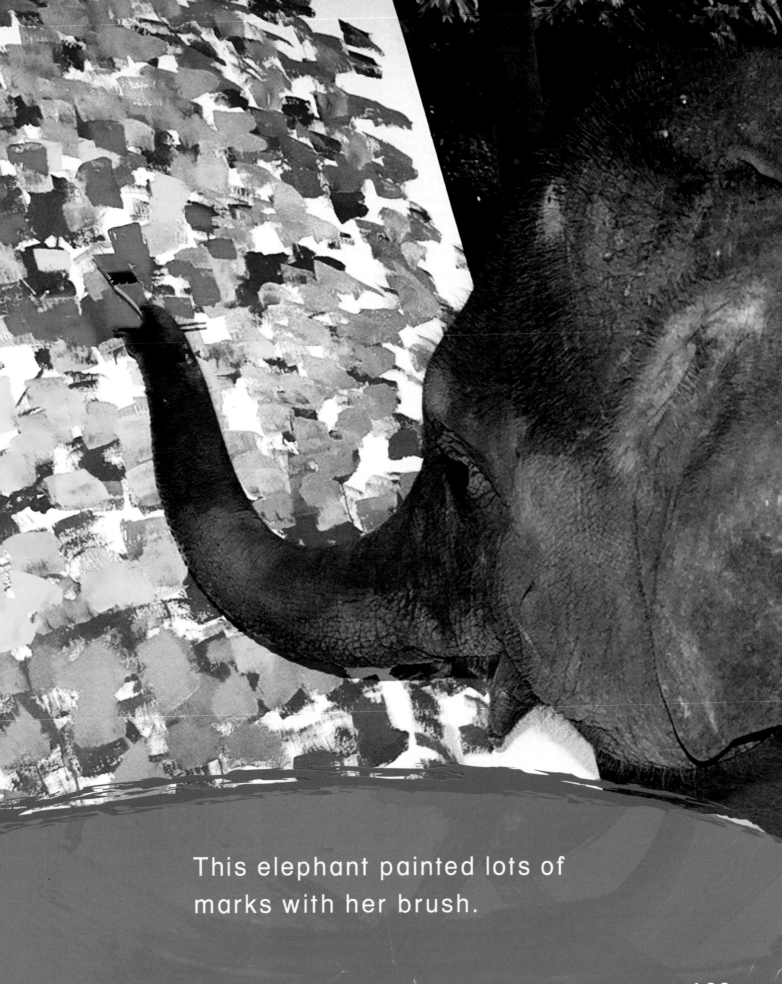

This elephant painted lots of marks with her brush.

Others liked lines and spots.
They made them thin and thick,
short and long, pink and black.

One painted simple flowers.

A little one just wanted to nibble
his brush.

People saw this art and said,
"It's so nice!"
They wanted to buy the art.
They hung it in their homes.

"Thank you for helping us!"
Ning said to the artist.
Now they all had new jobs.

Think Critically

1. Why was it a good idea for the elephants to learn to paint? MAIN IDEA

2. What is Lucky's home like? DETAILS

3. How does Ning feel when all the big trees are gone? Why? DRAW CONCLUSIONS

4. Think about the beginning and the end of this selection. How does Lucky's life change? MAKE INFERENCES

5.  **WRITE** Write about something else an elephant could learn to do.

   WRITING RESPONSE

 SS BENCHMARKS
LA.1.1.7.2 use background knowledge/supporting details; LA.1.1.7.3 retell the main idea; LA.1.1.7.4 identify supporting details; LA.1.4.2.1 write informational/ expository forms

Meet the Author/Photographer
Katya Arnold

Katya Arnold teaches art to children in New York—and to elephants in Asia! Her husband Alex is also an artist. Together, they helped the elephants create amazing paintings.

Some elephants painted for a long time. Others just played with the brushes. But they all liked to sneak snacks out of the artists' pockets with their trunks!

GO online www.harcourtschool.com/storytown

Science

An
Elephant's
Three
T's

Nonfiction Article

Teacher Read-Aloud

An Elephant's Three T's

Teeth

Animals that eat plants have flat teeth. Elephants use their flat teeth to chew leaves, twigs, fruit, and bark.

Tusks

Elephant tusks are long teeth. They are made of ivory. Elephants can use their tusks to help get food.

Trunk

Elephants breathe through their trunks. They also use their trunks to put food and water in their mouths. They can even take a shower.

Best of all, elephants use their trunks to give each other a hug!

Connections

Comparing Texts LA.1.2.1.5

1 What is the most interesting thing you learned from the selection and the article?

2 Tell about an elephant that you have seen. What did it do?

3 What is your favorite way to make pictures? Tell how you do it.

Can Elephants Paint?
by Katya Arnold

An Elephant's Three T's

Writing LA.1.1.7.3 LA.1.4.2.1

Write notes telling what you know about elephants. Then write sentences.

Elephants can pick up things with their strong trunks.

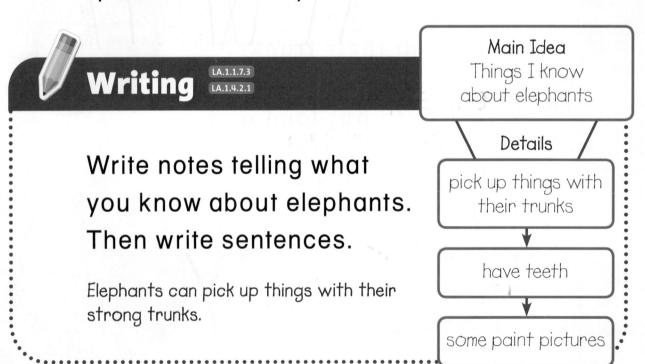

Main Idea
Things I know about elephants

Details

pick up things with their trunks

↓

have teeth

↓

some paint pictures

Phonics `LA.1.1.4.1`

Make and read new words.

Start with **little**.

Change **l** to **w** and **t** **t** to **g** **g**.

Change **w** to **g**.

Change **gigg** to **cand**.

Change **c** to **h**.

Fluency Practice `LA.1.1.5.1` `LA.1.1.5.2`

Read "Can Elephants Paint?" aloud to a partner. Pause when you see a comma or a period. Use your voice to show excitement when there is an exclamation point.

Let's paint, Lucky!

SS BENCHMARKS

LA.1.1.4.1 generate/blend sounds into words; LA.1.1.5.1 apply letter-sound knowledge to decode quickly and accurately;
LA.1.1.5.2 recognize high-frequency/familiar words; LA.1.1.7.3 retell the main idea; LA.1.2.1.5 respond to texts;
LA.1.4.2.1 write informational/expository forms

Contents

Lesson 18

1 Get Started Story

Shadow in the Snow

by Nancy Furstinger
illustrations by Jesse Reisch

2 Genre: Realistic Fiction

Snow Surprise

by Lisa Campbell Ernst

The Snowflake Man

3 Genre: Nonfiction Article

Phonics

Words with <u>ow</u> and <u>oa</u>

Words to Know

Review

play

day

tree

onto

eat

Shadow in the Snow

by Nancy Furstinger

illustrated by Jesse Reisch

"Follow me, Shadow,"
yells Jess. "Let's play
in the snow!"

"Look at that black crow,"
Jess grins. "He soaks up sun
and sings all day."

A rabbit rests by an oak tree.
Shadow sniffs the snow. He
thinks he is on a hunt.

Jess tucks her chin under her yellow
coat. Snow blows off a branch and
onto her hat. "Shadow!" she calls.

A rowboat sits on a pond. "In spring, we'll row that boat on the water," Jess tells Shadow.

Jess zips along a hilltop on her sled.
Shadow runs with Jess.

"Let's have a snack, Shadow. I will eat an apple muffin, and you can drink a bowl of milk. Then let's go back and play in the snow!"

Phonics Skill

Words with <u>ow</u> and <u>oa</u>

The letters **ow** can stand for the long **o** sound, as in the words **bowl** and **snow**.

bowl　　　　**snow**

The letters **oa** can also stand for the long **o** sound, as in the words **goat** and **road**.

goat　　　　**road**

**Look at each picture. Read the words.
Tell which word names the picture.**

toad

boat

coat

bowl

blow

bow

 www.harcourtschool.com/storytown

Read the sentences.

I put on my coat to go out.
I could see the wind blow the
trees. I could see snow on the
road. I was glad I had my coat.

SS BENCHMARKS
LA.1.1.4.1 generate/blend sounds into words; LA.1.1.4.2 identify vowel sounds/
consonant digraphs

our

pretty

surprise

over

three

mouse

216

There is lots of snow, and **our** yard looks pretty. I run out into the snow. I want to make a **surprise**.

Our dog runs so fast that he jumps **over** the steps! He runs with me into the snow. Then, he barks **three** times. Is Sport barking at a **mouse** or at some other animal?

www.harcourtschool.com/storytown

SS BENCHMARK
LA.1.1.4.5 recognize high-frequency words

Snow Surprise
by Lisa Campbell Ernst

Realistic Fiction

LA.1.2.1.1
LA.1.2.1.2
LA.1.2.1.3 **Genre Study**

Realistic fiction stories are made-up, but the events could happen in real life.

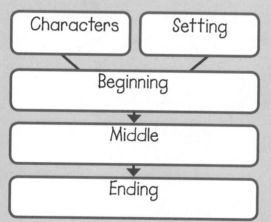

Characters | Setting

Beginning

Middle

Ending

LA.1.1.7.2 **Comprehension Strategy**

Monitor Comprehension: Make Inferences Use clues from what you are reading and what you already know to help you understand the story.

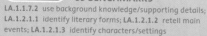 **SS BENCHMARKS**
LA.1.1.7.2 use background knowledge/supporting details;
LA.1.2.1.1 identify literary forms; LA.1.2.1.2 retell main
events; LA.1.2.1.3 identify characters/settings

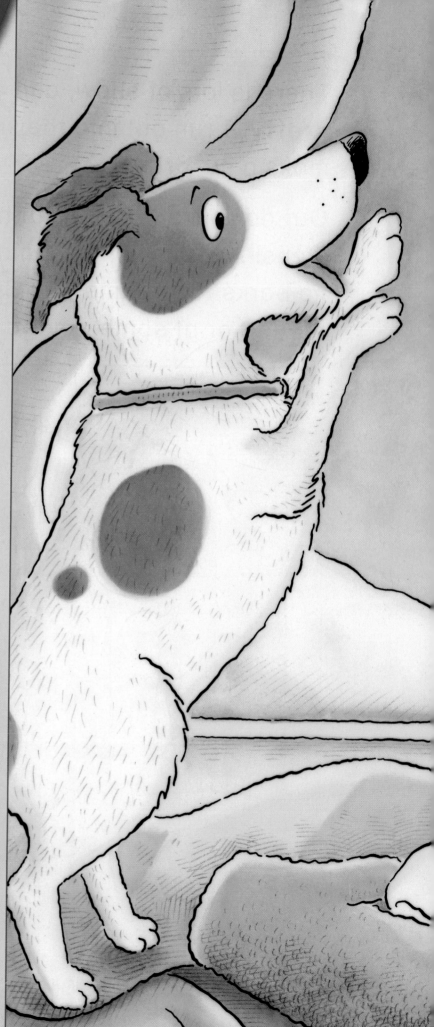

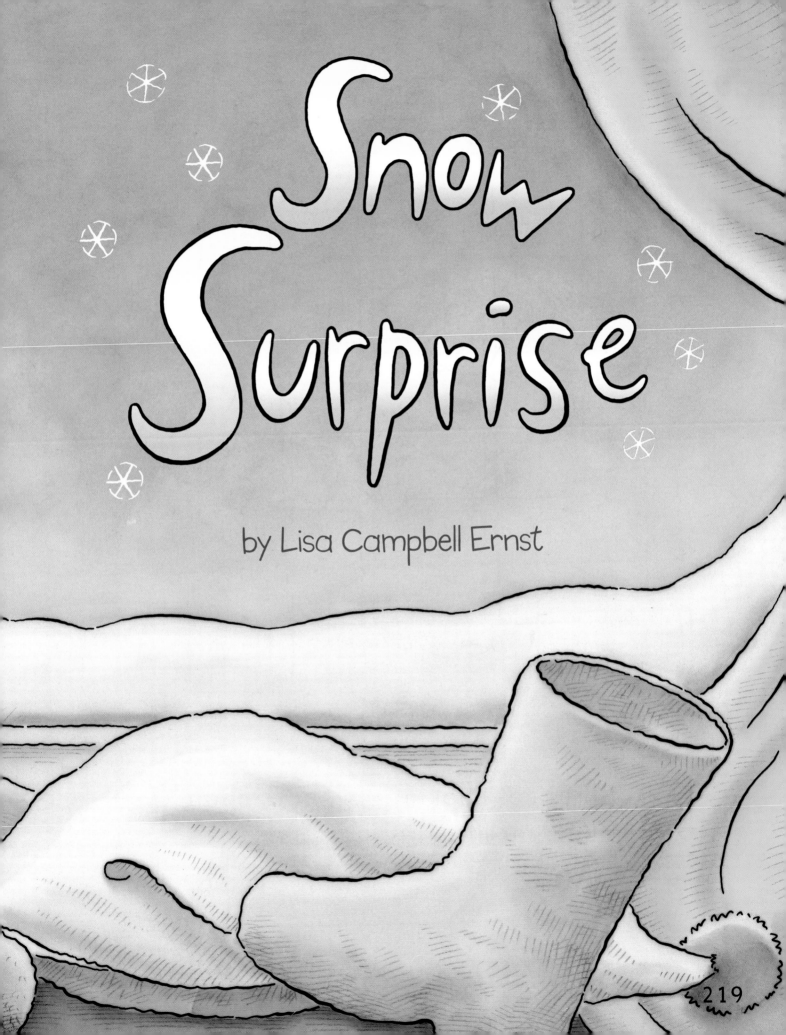

Snow Surprise

by Lisa Campbell Ernst

"Surprise! Look at the snow, Joan!"
yelled her little brother, Ben.

Joan looked out. The snow
was so pretty! Sport barked.

"I saw the snow first!
I saw the snow first!"
Ben sang.

221

Joan ran for her coat. "I'll show
you a snow surprise," she called to
Ben. Joan loaded her pockets with
all sorts of things.

"Don't look!" she said.
Then she ran out with Sport.

It was cold! Frost was on the porch. Joan jumped off and landed in the snow.

Sport ran and jumped in the snow, too. He nipped at the snow floating in the air.

"Come with me, Sport!" Joan called.

Joan packed snow into a small
ball. Then she started rolling
the ball.

"It's growing!" Joan yelled.

Joan made three snowballs. They were all in a row—big, bigger, and biggest.

Joan stacked the snowballs to make her snow surprise. She put one on top of the other.

She patted on more snow to fill
in the gaps. Sport barked at the
crows and other birds.

At last, Joan added the things from her pockets. She had apples, nuts, yellow corn, crusts of toast, and more.

Sport got sticks. Joan used them to make arms. She put food for the birds in bowls. Then she loaned her own hat and scarf to the snow surprise.

"Our snow surprise is perfect," Joan said to Sport. She ran in to get Ben.

Out in the yard, the birds saw corn and toast. The animals smelled nuts and apples.

What did Sport smell?
He smelled trouble!

In a flash, there <u>was</u> trouble.
The birds snatched the food. The
animals munched. It was a mad
dash for the snacks!

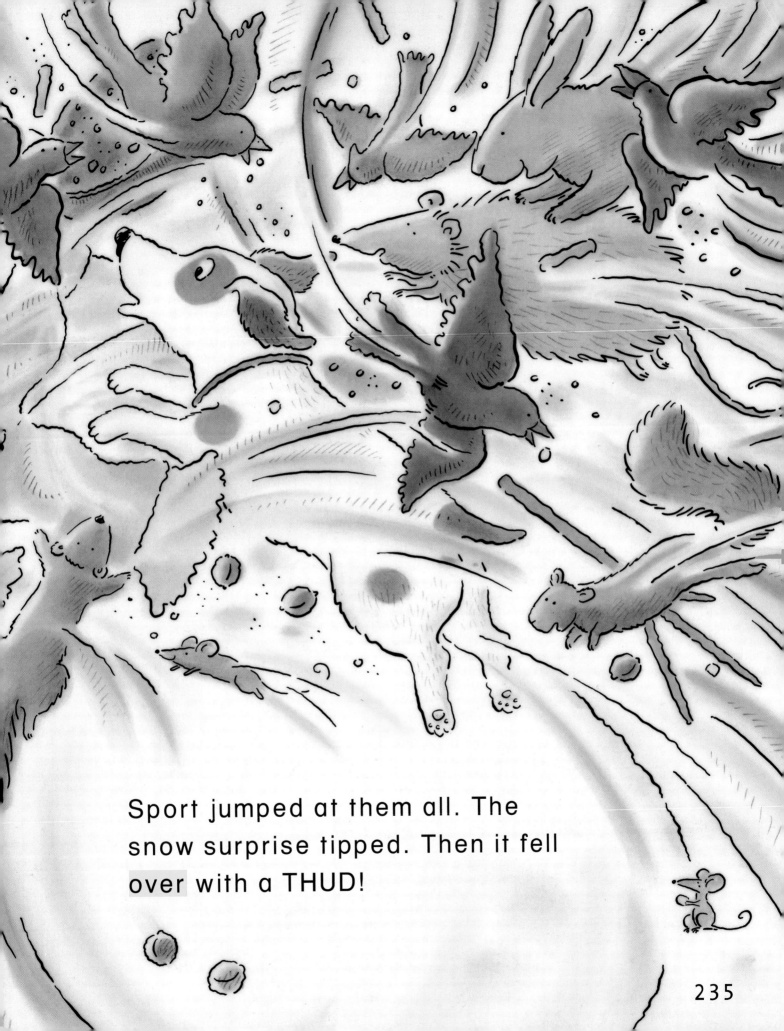

Sport jumped at them all. The snow surprise tipped. Then it fell over with a THUD!

Joan led Ben out to show him
the surprise. She gasped. It was
not there!

"Oh, no," Joan groaned.

Ben clapped his hands. "A mouse!" he sang. "It's a snow mouse!"

Joan looked again. It <u>was</u> a mouse.

"Surprise!" she said.

Think Critically

1 Why do you think the author wrote this story?  AUTHOR'S PURPOSE/POINT OF VIEW

2 What are the steps for making Joan's snow surprise? DETAILS

3 Do you think the animals are happy that Joan is making a snow surprise? Why or why not? DRAW CONCLUSIONS

4 Think about the ending. What do you think Joan and Ben will do next?

MAKE INFERENCES

5 READ THINK EXPLAIN **WRITE** Write about something you made to surprise someone, or about a time someone surprised you.

WRITING RESPONSE

FCAT ✓ **SS BENCHMARKS**

LA.1.1.7.4 identify supporting details; LA.1.1.7.6 sequence events; LA.1.1.7.8 identify author's purpose; LA.1.2.1.5 respond to texts; LA.1.4.2.1 write informational/ expository forms

238

Lisa Campbell Ernst

Lisa Campbell Ernst grew up in a family that loved books and sharing stories. So, she would draw pictures and make up stories about the animals in her neighborhood.

“I still love drawing animals! To know how to draw Sport, I watched my pets Fred and Elmo playing outside. I watched the wildlife in my backyard for the other animals, and my daughter Allison to draw Joan.”

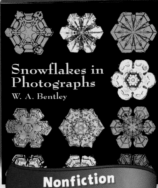

Snowflakes in Photographs
W. A. Bentley

Nonfiction

The Snowflake Man

Wilson Bentley *loved* snow! He loved looking at snowflakes, but they would melt. Then he found a way to keep his snowflakes. He took pictures of them!

Read what Wilson Bentley said about snow.

"I was born in 1865, and
I can't remember a time
I didn't love the snow."

▼ Wilson Bentley is using an old
camera to take his famous pictures.
He is known as "Snowflake Bentley."

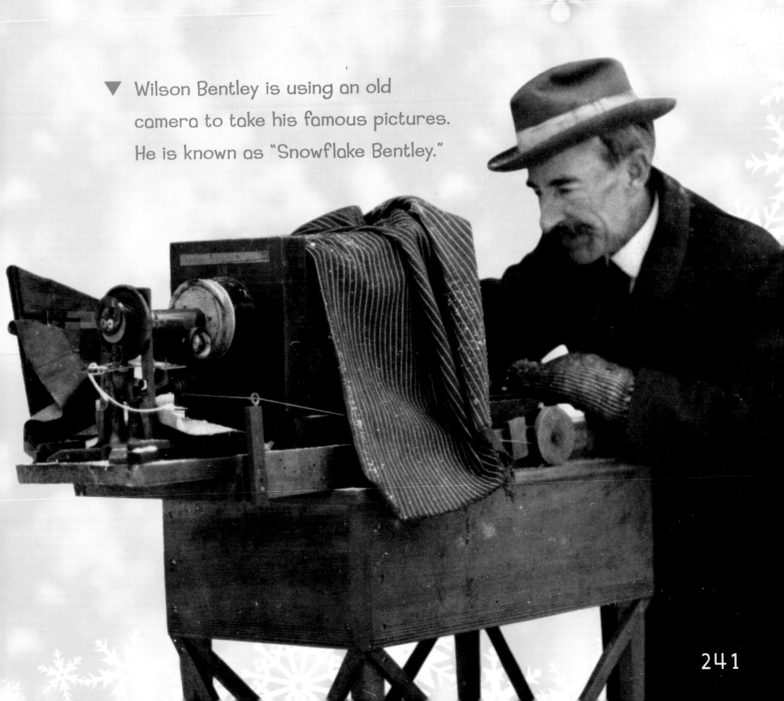

"A snowstorm is always so exciting to me. I never know when I am going to find some wonderful prize."

"You asked how I catch my crystals. I do it with this little wooden tray. It is painted black so that the flakes will show against it."

"Usually they have six sides or six branches. And the six sides will be exactly the same."

"Each snowflake is as different from its fellows as we are from each other."

Connections

Comparing Texts LA.1.2.1.5

1 What was the most interesting thing you learned about snow from "Snow Surprise" or "The Snowflake Man"?

2 What other things do people do in the snow for fun?

3 Tell about something you made that did not turn out the way you expected.

✏ Writing LA.1.4.2.4

Pretend that Joan made the snow surprise for you. Write a note to thank her for it.

> January 17, 20--
> Dear Joan,
>   Thank you for making the snow surprise for me. It looks like a giant mouse! How did you make it?
>   Your Pal,
>   Emma

Make and read new words.

Start with **slow**.

Change **s** **l** to **r**.

Change **w** to **a** **d**.

Change **r** to **t**.

Change **d** to **s** **t**.

Take turns reading pages of "Snow Surprise." Make the characters sound as if they are really talking to you.

"Come with me, Sport!"

SS BENCHMARKS
LA.1.1.4.1 generate/blend sounds into words; **LA.1.1.5.1** apply letter-sound knowledge to decode quickly and accurately; **LA.1.1.5.2** recognize high-frequency/familiar words; **LA.1.2.1.5** respond to texts; **LA.1.4.2.4** write basic communications (friendly letters, thank-you notes)

Glossary

What Is a Glossary?

A glossary can help you read a word. You can

look up the word and read it in a sentence.

Some words have a picture to help you.

gift   **Jill got a gift.**

A

air   **She can blow air to make bubbles.**

B

books   **Here is a stack of books.**

buy   **She will buy markers for school.**

carry   He can **carry** the water.

family   There are two children in my **family.**

fly   He can make it **fly.**

friends   Emma and Beth are good **friends.**

H

house   I see a tree by the **house.**

K

know   We **know** how to add.

L

loud   This animal has a **loud** roar.

money   She has **money** on her desk.

mouse   A **mouse** is a very small animal.

name   His dog's **name** is Spot.

nice   She is **nice** to help.

over   The ball went **over** his head.

paint   We have **paint** and brushes.

paper   This **paper** is pink.

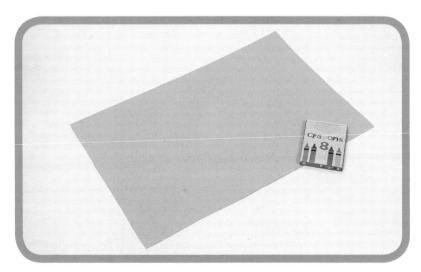

people   Many **people** went to the park.

play   Sal likes to **play** at the park.

pretty   The flowers are **pretty**.

R

---

rain   The **rain** fell hard.

read I **read** a book with Granddad.

room Jim has a clock in his **room.**

S

surprise The gift was a **surprise.**

three   Here are **three** flowers.

W

watch   They **watch** for the bus to come.

work   The birds **work** on their nest.

writing   She is **writing** a list.

Acknowledgments

For permission to reprint copyrighted material, grateful acknowledgment is made to the following sources:

Mari Evans: "I Can" from *Singing Black* by Mari Evans. Published by Reed Visuals, 1979.

Marian Reiner, on behalf of the Boulder Public Library Foundation: "Caterpillars" from *Cricket in a Thicket* by Aileen Fisher. Text copyright © 1963 by Aileen Fisher.

Photo Credits

Placement Key: (t) top; (b) bottom; (l) left; (r) right; (c) center; (bg) background; (fg) foreground; (i) inset

12 (c) Images.com/Corbis; 15 (b) Don Farrall / Getty Images; 24 Creatas Images/JupiterImages; 6 Petr RF/Shutterstock; 31 (inset) Peter J Bryant/ BPS/Stone/Getty Images; 41 (bg) Raul Touzon/National Geographic/ Getty Images; 42 (c) Photo 24/Brand X Pictures /JupiterImages; 53 (bl) Royalty Free/Corbis; 62 Ariel Skelley/Corbis; 62 Ingram Publishing /SuperStock; 62 Purestock /SuperStock; 63 Masterfile Royalty Free; 64 (t) image100/SuperStock; 93 (br) RubberBall Productions/PictureQuest; 140 David S April RF/Shutterstock; 102 Christopher Bissell/Stone/Getty Images; 103 Geoff Dann/Dorling Kindersley/Getty Images; 103 Markus Botzek/zefa/Corbis; 129 (br) Ariel Skelley/Blend Images/Picture Quest; 138 BananaStock/Alamy; 161 (c) © Gray Crabbe / Enlightened images; 161 (tc) © Tim Hursley / SuperStock; 161 (c) Ian Dagnall/Alamy; 161 (tc) Jeremy Woodhouse/Digital Vision/Getty Images; 165 (b) Art Wolfe/Getty Images; 176 Katya Arnold; 176 (t) tadija/Shutterstock; 200 (fg) Andy Rouse/NHPA; 201 (cr) Cris Haigh/Alamy; 201 (tr) Matthias Clamer/Getty Images; 201 (br) ZSSD/Minden Pictures; 202 (t) tadija RF/Shutterstock; 205 (l) Stockdisc/Getty Images; 214 (c) Allan Davey / Masterfile; 214 (c) Ray Ooms / Masterfile; 214 Eline Spek/Shutterstock; 215 Royalty-Free/Corbis; 215 SuperStock; 216 (t) Pepe Ramirez/ Shutterstock; 240- 242, 243-245 (t) Peter Wolf/ Wolf Multimedia Studio; 243 (br) Historic NWS Collection/National Oceanic and Atmospheric Administration/Department of Commerce; 246 (t) OlgaLis/Shutterstock. All other photos © Harcourt School Publishers. Harcourt photos provided by Harcourt Index, Harcourt IPR, and Harcourt Photographers: Weronica Ankarorn, Eric Camden, Doug DuKane, Ken Kinsie, April Riehm and Steve Williams.

Illustration Credits

Cover Art; Laura and Eric Ovresat, Artlab, Inc.

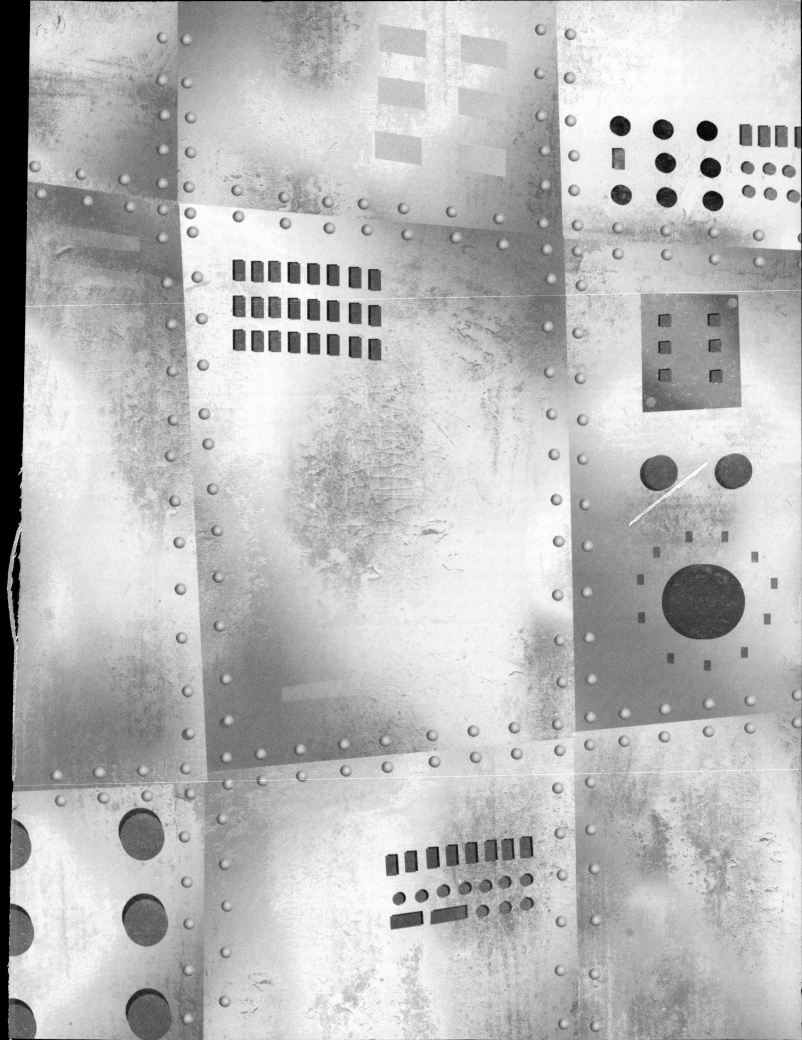

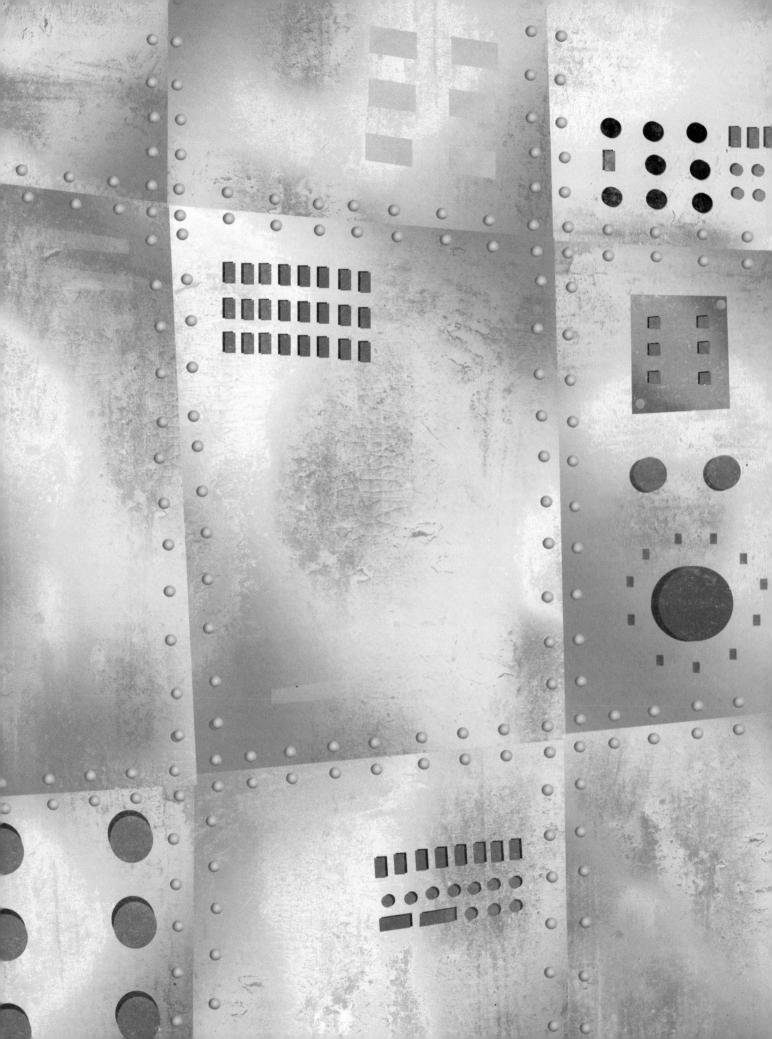